It's My State!

Nevada
The Silver State

Ruth Bjorklund, Terry Allen Hicks, and Ellen H. Todras

Cavendish Square

New York

Published in 2016 by Cavendish Square Publishing, LLC
243 5th Avenue, Suite 136, New York, NY 10016

Website: cavendishsq.com

This publication represents the opinions and views of the author based on his or her personal experience, knowledge, and
research. The information in this book serves as a general guide only. The author and publisher have used their best efforts in
preparing this book and disclaim liability rising directly or indirectly from the use and application of this book.

CPSIA Compliance Information: Batch #CW16CSQ

All websites were available and accurate when this book was sent to press.

Library of Congress Cataloging-in-Publication Data

Hicks, Terry Allan, author.
Nevada / Terry Allan Hicks, Ellen H. Todras, and Ruth Bjorklund.
pages cm. — (It's my state!)
Includes index.
ISBN 978-1-6271-3207-7 (hardcover) ISBN 978-1-6271-3209-1 (ebook)
1. Nevada—Juvenile literature. I. Todras, Ellen H., 1947- author. II. Bjorklund, Ruth, author. III. Title.

F841.3.H54 2016
979.3—dc23

2015027399

Editorial Director: David McNamara
Editor: Fletcher Doyle
Copy Editor: Rebecca Rohan
Art Director: Jeffrey Talbot
Designer: Stephanie Flecha
Senior Production Manager: Jennifer Ryder-Talbot
Production Editor: Renni Johnson
Photo Research: J8 Media

The photographs in this book are used by permission and through the courtesy of: Darren J. Bradley/Shutterstock.com, cover; Dcrjsr/File:Pinyon pine Pinus
Monophylla.jpg/Wikimedia Commons, 4; James Urbach/Superstock, 4; Tier und Naturfotografe/Superstock, 4; Minden Pictures/Superstock, 5; Heeb Christian/Prisma/
Superstock, 5; Wild Horizons/UIG/Getty Images, 5; Betty Wiley/Getty Images, 6; Lana Sundman/Alamy, 8; Westgraphix LLC, 10; Corey Rich/Aurora Open/Superstock,
11; Nomad/Superstock, 12; Larry Prosor/Superstock, 13; Ron Niebrugge/Alamy, 14; age fotostock/Superstock, 14; Michael DeFreitas/Robert Harding Picture Library/
Superstock, 14; Richard Cummins/Getty Images, 15; Pierre Camateros/File:Abandoned Rhyolite General Store.jpg/Wikimedia Commons, 15; Robert Harding Picture
Library /Super Stock, 15; Wolfgang Kaehler/Superstock, 17; Danita Delimont/Alamy, 18; Minden Pictures/Superstock, 19; Science Faction/Superstock, 20; George
Ostertag/age fotostock/Superstock, 20; Minden Pictures/Superstock, 20; Dennis W. Donohue/Shutterstock.com, 21; John Cancalosi/age fotostock/Superstock, 21;
Prisma/Superstock, 21; Kenkistler/Shutterstock.com, 22; Joseph Sohm/Shutterstock.com, 24; Universal Images Group/Superstock, 25; Bettmann/Corbis, 26; Everett
Collection/Superstock, 28; Fotosearch/Getty Images, 29; www.CleverPatch.com, 30; Everett Collection/Superstock, 32; Steve Vidler/Superstock, 34; F1 Online/
Superstock, 34; Niebrugge Images/Alamy, 35; EPoelzl/File:St. Charles-Muller's Hotel, Carson City, Nevada.jpg/Wikimedia Commons, 35; Sal Maimone/Superstock, 36;
Scheri/SZ Photo/The Image Works, 38; Allan Cash Picture Library/Alamy, 39; Science Faction/Superstock, 40; Millennium Images/Superstock, 41; William Stevenson/
Superstock, 44; ZUMA Wire Service/Alamy, 46; Everett Collection Inc./Alamy, 48; Bryan Steffy/Getty Images, 48; Mitchell Leff/Getty Images, 48; Transcendental
Graphics/Getty Images, 49; TopFoto/The Image Works, 49; Allstar Picture Library/Alamy, 49; AP Photo/Julie Jacobson, 51; Bloomberg/Getty Images, 52; Travel
Pictures Ltd/Superstock, 54; Steve Mansfield-Devine/Alamy, 54; Darren Carroll/Sports Illustrated/Getty Images, 55; Al Bello/Getty Images, 55; Karen Kasmauski/
Getty Images, 56; Matthew Heinrichs/Alamy, 58; age fotostock/Superstock, 59; AP Photo/Debra Reid, 61; Courtesy of the Nevada State Library, Archives and Public
Records, 62; United States Congress/File:Harry Reid official portrait 2009.jpg/Wikimedia Commons, 62; Ethan Miller/Getty Images, 62; Photograph ©2012 Deon
Reynolds Provided courtesy of Pattern Energy Group LP, 64; Bob Thomason/Getty Images, 66; Jim West/age fotostock/Superstock, 67; Ethan Miller/Reuters/Corbis,
68; imagebroker.net/Superstock, 68; age fotostock/Superstock, 69; Frank Parker/age fotostock/Superstock, 69; Sarsmis/Shutterstock.com, 70; Ethan Miller/Getty
Images, 71; Stephen A. Arce/NewSport/Corbis, 73; Christopher Santoro, 74 (map); Harry Thomas/Thinkstock, 75; Famartin/File:2015-01-15 14 39 17 View south along
U.S. Route 93 in Caliente,Nevada.jpg/Wikimedia Commons, 75; Christopher Santoro, 76 (seal and flag).

Printed in the United States of America

NEVADA
CONTENTS

★ State Trees: Single-Leaf Piñon (right) and the Bristlecone Pine

Nevada has two state trees, the single-leaf piñon and the bristlecone pine. The single-leaf piñon is a fragrant evergreen tree with gnarly branches that grows in sandy soil and rocky crevices. Bristlecone pines have twisted trunks and grow in high elevations. They are ancient trees.

★ State Bird: Mountain Bluebird

The mountain bluebird lives in meadows, sagebrush, mountains, and forests. The male is a brilliant turquoise blue. Often, they hover in midair to feed on insects. Male and female build their nest together in old trees, fence posts, and woodpecker holes.

★ State Animal: Desert Bighorn Sheep

Bighorn sheep are large **herbivores**, feeding on grasses and shrubs in rocky and remote areas. The males weigh 140 to 180 pounds (63.5 to 81.6 kilograms), while females weight 90 to 150 pounds (41 to 68 kg). The males have huge, curved horns and, during mating season, they fight for control of their band. Females have shorter horns.

NEVADA

★ State Flower: Sagebrush

Sagebrush, which has pale yellow flowers and a sweet smell, grows in harsh, dry places where few plants can grow. It is a low, woody shrub that flowers all summer. Sheep and cattle graze on sagebrush flowers, and the plant provides cover for small desert mammals and reptiles.

★ State Rock: Sandstone

Sandstone is found throughout Nevada. It can be yellow, red, brown, gray, black, pink, or white. Many of Nevada's peaks and dramatic cliffs are made of sandstone, including the Red Rock Canyon National **Conservation** Area. The state capitol and many historic buildings were built with quarried sandstone.

★ State Fossil: Ichthyosaur

A shallow, warm ocean covered Nevada more than 225 million years ago. The ichthyosaur, a now extinct reptile, once swam its waters. Many ichthyosaur **fossils**—the remains or traces of ancient plants or animals—have been discovered in sandstone rock at Berlin-Ichthyosaur State Park in central Nevada.

Valley of Fire State Park outside
Las Vegas glows in the sunset.

The Silver State

With snowcapped mountains, clear lakes, and large stretches of desert where wild horses roam, Nevada is one of the most beautiful states in the United States. For centuries, because the harsh climate made settling difficult, this area was nearly empty of inhabitants. But in recent years, millions of people have discovered Nevada, making it one of the nation's great tourist attractions and one of the fastest-growing states in population.

Nevada is a huge state—the seventh largest in the country—with a land area of 110,567 square miles (286,367 square kilometers). The state is divided into seventeen counties. Even though Nevada is a large state in land area, it ranks thirty-fifth in population. Its residents are not evenly distributed on the land. More than half of Nevadans live in the state's five most-populous cities.

The Sierra Nevada

Nevada, meaning snowfall in Spanish, takes its name from the Sierra Nevada, the great mountain range that runs north–south through parts of eastern California and western Nevada. The Sierra Nevada began to form about 150 million years ago, when huge masses of rock started to shift and push upward, and volcanoes spewed molten lava that cooled

The name Sierra Nevada comes from Spanish words meaning mountain and snowfall. The mountains are on Nevada's western border.

to form **granite** mountains. The tall peaks of the Sierra Nevada create a natural barrier between Nevada and California. The highest point in Nevada, Boundary Peak, at 13,147 feet (4,007 m), lies very close to the border between the two states.

Nevada has never been an easy place in which to live. The difficulty of traveling through the Sierra Nevada discouraged settlers for many years. Even today, with modern highways and four-wheel-drive vehicles, heavy snows sometimes cut off entire towns for days or even weeks at a time. And yet, Native Americans have made the Sierra Nevada their home for thousands of years. This is also the part of present-day Nevada where settlement by people of European descent began.

The strip of western Nevada in the shadow of the Sierra Nevada is where Reno, also known as the "biggest little city in the world," is located. Reno has only about 225,000 residents, but an average of more than 350,000 visitors travel to the city each

Nevada Borders

North:	Oregon Idaho
South:	California Arizona
East:	Arizona Utah
West:	California

month. Most of them come to enjoy an industry that has been the backbone of the state's economy for more than half a century: gambling.

But this part of Nevada has much more than roulette wheels, slot machines, and card tables to offer. Tourists remember Nevada's rich past in places such as Virginia City, which works hard to preserve the mining heritage that served as inspiration for one of the state's nicknames, the Silver State. More than a hundred years ago, when Virginia City was a very prosperous silver mining town, its population was around 30,000. Fewer than 1,000 people live there today.

Just 15 miles (24 km) south of Virginia City is another former mining center, Carson City. This tourist destination offers museums and restored buildings from pioneer days. Carson City is also Nevada's capital. Lawmakers meet here to decide on important issues facing the state.

West of Carson City, along the California-Nevada state line, is Lake Tahoe. The lake, famous for its sparkling blue water, covers 191 square miles (496 sq km). It is said that the water is so clear, you can sometimes see objects 75 feet (23 m) below the surface. Resorts on the shores of Lake Tahoe draw boaters, swimmers, and hikers in the summer. In the winter, skiers and snowboarders come to enjoy the deep powder at Mount Rose or Diamond Peak.

The Great Basin

Most of Nevada is in a region known as the Great Basin, about 190,000 square miles (492,000 sq km) in size. The Great Basin stretches from the foothills of the Sierra Nevada, on the state's western border, all the way to the Rocky Mountains, on Nevada's eastern border. This low-lying area was formed millions of years ago, when movements within Earth raised the surrounding areas. The Great Basin is shaped like a huge bowl, which is how it got its name. It is known for its unusual drainage system. Rivers and streams flowing into the Great Basin from the surrounding mountains end in low, marshy areas called sinks, or in stretches of dry, cracked clay called playas.

End of the Line

The 190,000 square miles [482,000 sq km] of the Great Basin drains inside itself. All water that enters—from rivers, rain, and snow—either evaporates, sinks underground, or settles into lakes. There are no outlets and no Great Basin water ever reaches the ocean.

NEVADA
COUNTY MAP

HUMBOLDT

ELKO

WASHOE

PERSHING

LANDER

EUREKA

WHITE PINE

STOREY

CHURCHILL

CARSON CITY

LYON

DOUGLAS

MINERAL

NYE

ESMERALDA

LINCOLN

CLARK

NEVADA

POPULATION BY COUNTY

Carson City	52,274	Lincoln	5,345
Churchill	24,877	Lyon	51,980
Clark	1,951,269	Mineral	4,772
Douglas	46,997	Nye	43,946
Elko	48,818	Pershing	6,753
Esmeralda	783	Storey	4,010
Eureka	1,987	Washoe	421,407
Humboldt	16,528	White Pine	10,030
Lander	5,775		

Source: US Bureau of the Census, 2010

Hikers climb a slope in the Great Basin National Park in eastern Nevada.

Mount Grant and Walker Lake are located in the beautiful Great Basin.

Nevada has more than a dozen volcanic areas in the Great Basin. The best known is the Lunar Crater Volcanic Field. It is more than 100 square miles (260 sq km) in size, located at the southern end of the Pancake Range mountains. The 430-foot-deep (130 m) Lunar Crater has been designated a National Natural Landmark.

The Great Basin also includes part of the Mojave Desert. This desert—the hottest and driest in the United States—covers more than 25,000 square miles (65,000 sq km) in southern Nevada and southeastern California. Desert bighorn sheep, desert tortoises, and jackrabbits live in much of the sparsely populated Mojave. The city of Las Vegas lies in this arid region as well.

The northern section of Nevada is "cowboy country," where many ranchers still drive their herds on horseback. Sometimes, ranchers and their herds stop traffic on the highways on the way to and from the ranches. The area around Elko, in the northeastern corner of the state, also has huge open-pit mining operations. The region has some of the largest gold deposits in the world.

Stretching south from cowboy country is a huge expanse of flatlands. Much of this area is semidesert—dry land where only the toughest plants and animals can survive. Cutting across this area are more than a hundred small, steep-sided mountain ranges that run from north to south. Very few people live here, and some counties are almost uninhabited. A stretch of Highway 50, outside Fallon, is sometimes called "the loneliest road in America," because people can drive parts of it for hours without seeing any other human beings. But this does not mean there is no human activity in the Nevada countryside. The federal government owns huge stretches of the Silver State, which it uses for many different purposes, such as designing ways to dispose of dangerous materials. Why are parts of Nevada so empty? Large areas of the state just do not have enough water to support a large population.

The Humboldt River is the largest river in Nevada, flowing from east to west for a distance of about 300 miles (500 km). The river begins in the mountains of the Humboldt-Toiyabe National Forest and ends in Humboldt Sink, a dry lakebed with no outlet. Settlers heading west to California in the 1800s traveled on a trail along the river. Today, drivers follow a similar route on Interstate 80.

Lake Tahoe is high in the Sierra Nevada mountain range—6,229 feet (1,899 m) above sea level. Located partly in Nevada and partly in California, it is one of the deepest, clearest lakes in the world. The lake's lowest spot is 1,645 feet (501 m) down. Lake Tahoe never freezes over, due partly to its size and partly to currents that keep the water moving.

The Humboldt River ends in a dry lakebed, so none of its water reaches an ocean.

Great Basin National Park

Lake Tahoe

Mark Twain Museum

1. Great Basin National Park

Mount Wheeler rises 13,063 feet (3,981 m) over Great Basin National Park, which is near Baker. Mountains, streams, lakes, glaciers, caves, and marshlands are home to a variety of fish, mammals, and birds.

2. Lake Mead National Recreation Area

The recreation area covers 1.5 million acres (607,028 ha) of desert landscape in Nevada and Arizona. Lake Mead is the largest man-made lake in the United States at 247 square miles (640 sq km). It was created in 1935 when the Hoover Dam was built on the Colorado River.

3. Lake Tahoe

Freel Peak towers over Lake Tahoe, which is 1,645 feet (501 m) deep and covers 191 square miles (495 sq km). Tourists flock to the bright blue lake and surrounding snow-covered peaks to enjoy their recreational opportunities.

4. Mark Twain Museum

Samuel Clemens used the pen name Mark Twain for the first time while working as a reporter at the *Territorial Enterprise* in Virginia City. The museum contains the newspaper's furnishings and pressroom equipment, and the chair and desk used by Twain.

5. National Wild Horse and Burro Center

Nevada is home to most of the nation's wild horses and burros, descendants of animals abandoned in the 1820s. The largest adoption facility is the National Wild Horse and Burro Center in Palomino Valley.

6. Nevada State Museum

The state museum in the capital, Carson City, showcases Nevada's past. There are many exhibits on Nevada history, including geology, Native Americans, and replicas of a ghost town and a silver mine.

7. Pahranagat National Wildlife Refuge

This refuge near Alamo receives only 6.4 inches (16.25 cm) of rain a year. Yet many lakes and wetlands dot the refuge's 5,380 acres (2,177 ha). The wetlands are home to ducks, geese, eagles, and migratory birds, as well as catfish, tortoises, rattlesnakes, and mule deer.

8. Rhyolite

The ghost town of Rhyolite, which is near Beatty, was settled in 1904. Gold mining brought ten thousand people to town, which prospered until a banking crash in 1907. The last resident died in 1924, but many historic buildings still stand.

9. Ruby Mountains Wilderness

The remote Ruby Mountains are high, snow-covered peaks formed of granite. Peaks higher than 10,000 feet (3,048 m) tower over 100 miles (161 km) of canyons, lakes, and valleys. Garnets, not rubies, are found in the rock.

10. Valley of Fire State Park

The rugged, red sandstone landscape of the Valley of Fire near Overton was once home to dinosaurs. Early people settled there three thousand years ago. Visitors can view fossils as well as ancient rock drawings carved by early people.

Nevada State Museum

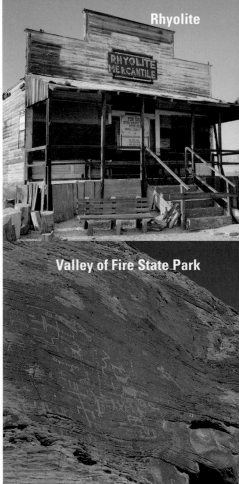

Rhyolite

Valley of Fire State Park

A huge body of water can be found in the southern Nevada desert. The water comes from the Hoover Dam, located along the Nevada-Arizona border. This enormous concrete dam controls the flooding of the Colorado River and supplies precious water for homes and farms. When the Hoover Dam was built in the 1930s, it created Lake Mead, a reservoir in the desert. This body of water, located partly in Nevada and partly in Arizona, is one of the largest artificial lakes in the world. It covers about 157,900 acres (63,900 hectares).

Today, millions of people come every year to enjoy this clear blue lake in the middle of the bone-dry desert. Power generators at the Hoover Dam also produce large amounts of electricity. That is a good thing because rising from the desert only about 25 miles (40 km) to the northwest are the glittering, neon-lit towers of Las Vegas.

Las Vegas, located in southern Nevada, is the largest city in the state. It is home to the world-famous Las Vegas Strip—a stretch of 4 miles (6 km) of road lined with hotels and casinos. Las Vegas is often called the Entertainment Capital of the World. Many singers, dancers, circus professionals, and other entertainers perform on the stages of this city.

Many people have come to the Las Vegas area to live and work. In the decade from 2000 to 2010, it was the fastest-growing metropolitan area in the United States, according to the US Census Bureau, even though it was hit hard by the economic downturn, or recession, that began in late 2007. What was once a small, sleepy town now extends far out into what had been uninhabitable desert.

Climate

The Silver State has one of the world's most extreme climates. Nevada is the driest state in the country. Its average precipitation totals just 7 inches (18 centimeters) a year. The national average is 40 inches (102 cm). Yet some parts of the Sierra Nevada get more than 80 inches (200 cm) of precipitation in a year. And in many parts of the state, sudden thunderstorms send **flash floods** racing down on unsuspecting hikers.

Temperatures in the state also vary. The temperature in the south can shift wildly in a single day, from 80 degrees Fahrenheit (27 degrees Celsius) in the afternoon to only a few degrees above

Unique Fauna and Flora

Ash Meadows National Wildlife Refuge is a rare desert oasis that is home to more than twenty-five endemic species, which are plants [flora] and animals [fauna] that live nowhere else in the world.

Some plants thrive in the Red Rock Canyon National Conservation Area despite a lack of rainfall.

freezing—32°F (0°C)—at night. The desert town of Laughlin recorded a blistering 125°F (52°C) on June 29, 1994. But Nevada also experiences cold temperatures. The coldest temperature recorded was on January 8, 1937, when thermometers in the northern town of San Jacinto fell to −50°F (−46°C).

Despite these wide variations in temperature and precipitation, Nevada's climate is very consistent in one way: There is almost always a lot of sunlight. In fact, the state's southern desert can get as many as 320 sunny days in a year.

Wild Nevada

Many plants and animals survive—and even thrive— in Nevada, despite the harsh environment. Even in the parched desert, sagebrush, yucca, Joshua trees, and more than two dozen types of cactus can be found. In places in the state where water is more plentiful, Indian paintbrush, shooting stars, and yellow and white violets dot the countryside.

Many parts of the Silver State are almost completely treeless, but juniper, pine, and fir trees grow in the mountains. Ancient bristlecone pines cling to the steep slopes of Wheeler Peak, in Great Basin National Park. All over the state, wherever there is a little water, alder, chokecherry, and cottonwood trees grow. In the autumn, their leaves turn yellow, bringing a welcome touch of color to the landscape.

Among the large animals in Nevada are bighorn sheep, pronghorns (which are sometimes called antelope), elk, mule deer, mustangs, and small donkeys called burros. Coyotes and bobcats are also common. Smaller animals include cottontail rabbits, foxes, and porcupines. Nevada also has plenty of reptiles, including lizards and snakes, such as

Wildflowers decorate the slopes of the Humboldt-Toiyabe National Forest.

the Western fence lizard, the rattlesnake, and the poisonous Gila monster.

Many parts of Nevada are growing so fast that humans sometimes come into conflict with wildlife. Coyotes have been known to drink from suburban swimming pools, and rattlesnakes sometimes sleep under cars on hot days.

Nevada's lakes and rivers are filled with fish that sport fishers love to catch and eat, including largemouth bass, perch, and trout. Many birds—including a number of water birds, such as ducks, geese, and pelicans—fill Nevada's skies. Nevada is also home to birds of prey such as falcons, bald and golden eagles, and owls, as well as smaller birds such as bluebirds, hummingbirds, swallows, and doves.

Wildlife at Risk

Nevada's fast-growing human population threatens the habitats of some of its plants and animals. An animal or plant type, or species, is considered threatened when it is at risk of becoming endangered. When a species is endangered, it is at risk of dying out in its range or a large area of its range. When a species is threatened, it is at risk of becoming endangered.

Nevada has twenty-seven endangered and sixteen threatened species. The state reptile, the desert tortoise, is threatened. This reptile, the largest in the southwestern United States, can live more than seventy years. It survives in the harsh conditions of southern

The desert tortoise is among the sixteen threatened species in Nevada.

Nevada—hot in the summer, cold in the winter—by living in underground burrows. Nevada's desert tortoise population has fallen sharply in recent years. Some people hunt the animals illegally, and others hit them accidentally with their cars.

The cui-ui (pronounced kwee-wee), a rare fish found only in Pyramid Lake, has been listed as an endangered species since 1967. Other endangered animals in Nevada include the gray wolf, the Southwestern willow flycatcher, and many more kinds of fish. Endangered plants include the herbs steamboat buckwheat and Amargosa niterwort.

The Nevada Fish and Wildlife Office is a state agency whose mission is to conserve Nevada's natural biological diversity. The agency works with many partners to prevent native species throughout the state from dying out and to help increase the populations of endangered species.

Many Nevadans are concerned about the need to protect their unique natural environment. For example, the state legislature has passed important laws to protect Nevada's wild horses, keep Lake Tahoe free from pollution, and set aside large wilderness areas as nature preserves. The people of Nevada are determined to protect their clean air and valuable water from the damaging effects of pollution and development.

American White Pelican

Bristlecone Pine

Gila Monster

1. American White Pelican

Every spring, thousands of American white pelicans descend on the streams and lakes of western Nevada, especially Pyramid Lake, to breed. The pelicans stand as much as 50 inches (125 cm) high. Their wingspan can measure 110 inches (280 cm).

2. Bristlecone Pine

The bristlecone has sharp needles and prickly cones and grows in the mountains of Nevada and California. In 1964, loggers cut down a bristlecone pine that was about four thousand years old.

3. Chuckwalla Lizard

Chuckwallas are mostly gray with loose skin on their necks. Snout to tail, they measure about 16 inches (42 cm). Chuckwallas live in the Great Basin and eat flowers, leaves, and fruit. In winter, chuckwallas hibernate.

4. Desert Tortoise

The threatened desert tortoise burrows in the sand or hides under creosote bushes. It feeds in the fall on desert plants, which provide water. An adult can weigh up to 17 pounds (8 kg). If it abandons its home, burrowing owls move in.

5. Gila Monster

The largest lizard in North America is one of only two poisonous lizards in the world. It feeds on birds, lizards, and their eggs, and swallows its prey whole. Is has thick legs for digging, and a keen sense of smell and hearing.

NEVADA ★ ★ ★ ★ ★

6. Greasewood

Greasewood is a thorny shrub, 3 to 7 feet (0.9 to 2.1 m) tall, which grows in salty soil at high elevations. It has two flowers—pink and green—and provides food and shelter for wildlife.

7. Pronghorn Antelope

Desert-dwelling pronghorns are the fastest running hoofed animals in North America, reaching speeds up to 60 miles per hour (97 kmh). They have a field of vision of nearly 360 degrees and can spot predators at great distances. Males and females have horns that they shed each year.

8. Sidewinder

The poisonous sidewinder, one of seven rattlesnake species in Nevada, is named for the unusual way it moves. It moves sideways in a looping motion, leaving a distinctive S-shaped mark in the sand.

9. Wild Horse

In Nevada's pioneer days, horses escaped or were abandoned. Often called mustangs, they traveled in herds. As many as 2,500 of these horses roam the state's wide-open spaces.

10. Yucca

Yuccas are tall plants that grow throughout the southern Nevada desert. They have white or purple flowers and tall, spiky leaves that store water for use during dry periods. Native Americans ate the plant's flowers and leaves. Its roots can be made into soap.

Pronghorn Antelope

Sidewinder

Wild Horses

The discovery of gold brought many people to Nevada, but mines were abandoned when large amounts of silver were found.

From the Beginning

A harsh climate and mostly dry, rugged terrain make it challenging to live in the Silver State. Yet Native Americans have lived in the region for thousands of years, and other groups have been coming since the late 1700s.

The First Nevadans

The first people who lived in the area that includes present-day Nevada were early Native Americans, now known as **Paleo**-Indians. They are believed to have been descendants of people who crossed a land bridge that once connected Asia and North America tens of thousands of years ago. Over time, they spread out all over the Americas. The Paleo-Indians left behind many traces of their way of life, including stone weapons, baskets, and sandals. They also left behind rock carvings called petroglyphs. These artifacts show that the Paleo-Indians were living in the area as early as 10,000 BCE.

Then, between 300 BCE and 100 CE, a different group of Native American people, known as the Ancestral Puebloans (Anasazi), came to the region. It is not clear where this group came from. By about 700 CE, the Ancestral Puebloans were building communal dwellings called pueblos in several areas of the Southwest. The elaborate multistoried buildings, made out of sun-dried clay bricks, had as many as one hundred rooms.

The largest Ancestral Puebloan community may have been home to almost twenty thousand people.

The Ancestral Puebloans were farmers. They built dams on the rivers to irrigate, or bring water to, their fields of beans, corn, and squash. They were skilled artists who created beautiful black-and-white pottery and intricately woven baskets that are often included in museum collections.

By about 1150 CE, these remarkable people simply disappeared. Did famine, or drought, or war with neighboring Native Americans drive them out? The question has fascinated archaeologists and historians for many years, but nobody knows the answer.

During the early sixteenth century, the region that includes present-day Nevada was inhabited by Native Americans unrelated to the Ancestral Puebloans. The Northern Paiute lived in what is now western Nevada, while the Southern Paiute lived in the southeastern portion. The Shoshone made their homes in the eastern and central sections of present-day Nevada. The Washoe lived in the Lake Tahoe region.

Most of these peoples were nomadic hunters and gatherers. They traveled across the mountains and deserts in search of food. They followed herds of animals and hunted pronghorns and bighorn sheep. They also trapped rabbits and water birds, and they ate pine nuts and other plants. The Native American way of life remained unchanged for

Early Native Americans left behind petroglyphs at Atlatl Rock.

centuries, until European explorers and settlers began to arrive.

Exploration

The first European explorer to set foot in the region was probably Father Francisco Garcés, a Spanish priest who passed through while traveling from New Mexico to California in 1776. The Spaniards claimed the region that now includes Nevada as theirs, but they never really established settlements there. In 1821, when Mexico gained its independence from Spain, what is now Nevada became part of Mexico.

Other explorers passed through the area in the early 1800s, but they never stayed long. In 1827, Jedediah Smith, an American mountain man, led a party of fur trappers from today's

John Charles Frémont crossed and mapped Nevada in the 1840s.

Utah on the difficult journey across Nevada to California and back again. John Charles Frémont, a US Army officer and mapmaker, crisscrossed present-day Nevada in 1843 and 1844. He named the Carson River after his guide, the frontiersman Christopher "Kit" Carson.

The Old Spanish Trail, which cuts through southern Nevada, was one of the earliest routes west to Southern California. It linked Santa Fe, New Mexico, and Los Angeles, California, at a time when the Southwest belonged to Mexico. Between 1830 and 1840, Mexican and American traders used mule trains on the Old Spanish Trail to bring woolen goods to California. They returned with mules and horses for the Missouri and New Mexico markets.

The Native People

The largest Native American tribes of Nevada are the Paiute, Western Shoshone, Washoe, and Walapai. Each belonged to larger groups that ranged across the Western Plains, the Southwest deserts, and the Sierra Nevada mountains.

Tribes shared similar lifestyles. Men hunted deer, antelope, and small game, such as rabbits, and some hunted buffalo. They used bows, arrows, and spears, which were also used when men went to war. Some were fishers who used nets and fish traps. Women gathered roots, piñon nuts, seeds, and fruits. Women cooked, cleaned, and tended to their children. Children helped with daily chores, and mothers carried their babies on their backs in cradleboards. Many lived in **wickiups**, which are dome-shaped homes made of woven grass. Some bands traveled following herds of buffalo and lived in tepees, which are easier to move than wickiups. The women packed and unpacked the families' tepees and could move an entire village in an hour. Men wore breechcloth and leggings, and sometimes tied a decorative apron around their waist. Women usually wore animal hide dresses. In winter, all wore heavy shirts made of animal hides. They decorated special garments with shells, beads, and animal teeth.

Intricate woven baskets, such as the one shown in this 1933 photograph, are part of the Paiute tradition.

When the European-Americans encountered the native people, they found groups that had built strong communities, were fiercely loyal to each other, and worked together for survival. The first outsiders were Spanish soldiers looking for gold, Christian missionaries, and fur traders. Later, settlers passed through on their way to California and Oregon. They introduced guns, knives, and horses. Conflicts between Native bands and European settlers were deadly. Europeans also brought diseases that sickened the native people, and thousands of people died. The newcomers slaughtered the buffalo, leaving the native people without an important source for food, clothing, and building material. Tribes who depended on fishing in Lake Tahoe saw their livelihood overrun as newcomers began commercial fishing.

There are twenty federally recognized Native American bands living in Nevada today, most belonging to the Shoshone and Paiute tribes. There are eight **reservation** lands and thirty-two Native American colonies, each with its own tribal government.

Spotlight on The Paiute Tribe

Nevada is home to a Northern Paiute tribe and a Southern Paiute tribe. Both belong to a larger group of Paiute people living in Oregon, California, Idaho, Utah, and Arizona. Their name means "traveling back and forth."

Homes: Most Paiute bands lived in wickiups. Eastern groups built tepees. They moved often to follow wandering buffalo herds. When villagers moved, they took down their tepees and packed them and their other belongings onto a wooden sled called a travois. In earlier times, dogs pulled the travois, later the people used horses.

Food: Men hunted deer, antelope, and sometimes buffalo. Women gathered nuts, seeds, and fruit. Some were fishers who caught fish with nets and fish traps. They made reed boats.

Weapons and Tools: Men crafted spears, bows, and arrows. After the European-Americans arrived, they also used knives and rifles. Paiute people wove baskets and made pottery.

Clothing: Men wore breechcloth and leggings. Women wore deerskin dresses. Special clothing was decorated with fringe, beads, shells, and animal teeth. Men and women wore their hair long—loose or in braids. Many women wore woven "basket hats" and had facial tattoos.

Government: Each band had a chief who oversaw a council of elders. Chiefs passed their authority down to their sons. Today, tribal chiefs can be a man or a woman, and they are elected by the people.

Fun and Games: Paiute children and adults enjoyed footraces and a baseball-like game called shinny. Gambling games with dice and sticks were popular.

Miners removed millions of dollars of gold and silver from the Comstock Lode.

Settling the West

In 1846, the United States went to war with Mexico. The United States won the Mexican-American War, and the Treaty of Guadalupe Hidalgo officially ended the war in 1848. This agreement gave the United States control of most of the Southwest, including the land that is now Nevada. By then, thousands of American settlers were already headed west in wagon trains, to settle in Oregon and California. Beginning in 1849, even more came after gold was discovered at Sutter's Mill in Northern California. People poured into the California gold fields. Many of them used a route that passed through present-day Nevada. It was a long and dangerous trip.

In 1850, the US Congress created the Utah Territory—a large area of land that included most of present-day Nevada. Some of the first white settlers in this territory were members of a religious group known as the Mormons. They belonged to the Church of Jesus Christ of Latter-day Saints. Mormons began settling there with the goal of practicing their religion in peace. One group of Mormons founded a trading post called Mormon Station in the Carson Valley in 1851. It was the first permanent settlement by people of European descent in the land that would become Nevada.

In 1859, two prospectors found an enormous vein of gold running beneath the Sierra Nevada. Before they could file their claim to the land, they died. Another prospector, Henry Comstock, swore he owned the land where they had found the gold. Although he sold his claim and died a poor man, the find is called the Comstock Lode.

The discovery set off another gold rush, but the prospectors working the Comstock soon made an even more amazing discovery. The gold they were digging up was mixed with a blue-black "mud." They complained about the mud, until someone realized it contained silver. The silver was worth far more than the original gold. It was, in fact, the richest silver deposit in the United States.

When the news of the silver strike reached others, even more fortune seekers began flooding into the region. Scratching for silver in the rocky ground was hard, dirty, dangerous work. Many men died from mining accidents, disease, or harsh weather. The 1859–1860 winter was especially severe. Heavy snow closed the Sierra Nevada passes, and food supplies could not get through. The silver fields were also dangerous because they were lawless places. Disputes were often settled with fists, knives, or guns.

Despite these hardships, entire towns grew up practically overnight. Virginia City, which had been home to little more than a few prospectors in tents in 1859, had a population of more than fourteen thousand by 1870. The city even had its own newspaper,

This photo of Virginia City in 1880, which shows churches, mills, and schools, reveals how much progress the region made just twenty-one years after gold was found.

Making a Native American Dream Catcher

Many western Native American tribes wove decorative dream catchers, whose purpose is to catch a sleeping human's bad dreams.

What You Need

Paper plate

Scissors

Hole punch

96 inches (244 cm) of yarn

Tape

Beads

Three Feathers

Markers

Paint (any color)

Ruler

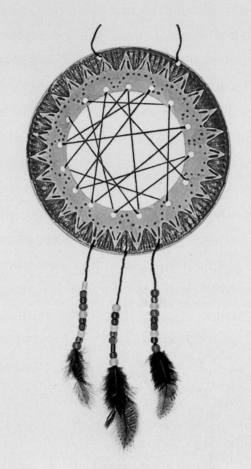

What To Do

- Cut about a 5-inch (13 cm) circle from the center of the paper plate, leaving the outer rim of the plate intact.
- Paint the rim
- Use the hole punch to make holes every inch around the inner part of the ring.
- Use markers to decorate the ring with Native American designs.
- Cut the yarn into five pieces: one piece measuring 48 inches (122 cm), four pieces measuring 12 inches (30.5 cm) each.
- Weave the long piece of yarn back and forth through the holes in the ring to create a web.
- Tape the ends of the yarn to the back of the ring.
- Make two holes at the top of the ring to hang the dream catcher. String a couple of beads onto one of the 12-inch (30.5 cm) pieces of yarn. Run the yarn through the holes and knot the ends.
- Use the hole punch and make three holes about an inch apart along the bottom of the dream catcher. Feed a 12-inch (30.5 cm) piece of yarn through each hole. On the back side, tie a big knot so the yarn does not fall out of the hole. String beads onto the yarn and tape a feather onto the end.
- Trim excess yarn with scissors.
- Hang near your bed and let the dream catcher catch all your bad dreams!

the *Territorial Enterprise*. A young reporter for the Enterprise, Samuel Clemens, later became world famous as Mark Twain, author of *The Adventures of Tom Sawyer* and The *Adventures of Huckleberry Finn*. Twain also published a book about his experiences in the West, including an account of the silver strike and of people's passion for the beautiful metal.

The silver rush and the increase in white settlement brought trouble for the region's Native Americans. The prospectors often stole the native people's land, hunted their game, and cut down the trees that the native people used for tools, shelter, and food. This sometimes led to violence between the two groups. In 1860, a group of Paiute men, angered by the kidnapping of two young girls from their village, killed three white men. The white settlers put together a group to fight the Paiute. But the Paiute ambushed them near Pyramid Lake. Seventy-six settlers were killed, in the first engagement of what came to be called the Pyramid Lake War. The settlers recovered and, aided by US Army troops, killed about 160 Paiute. The war lasted only a few months, and it ended Native American resistance in Nevada forever. The federal government forced the Native Americans of Nevada to move to reservations that had been set aside for them. One Nevada group, the Northern Paiute, refused to live on a reservation and settled on wilderness lands in what is now southern Utah instead.

On March 2, 1861, the government created the Nevada Territory, separate from the Utah Territory. Carson City served as the territorial capital, and President Lincoln named Orion Clemens the first and only Secretary of the Nevada Territory. He brought his famous brother, Samuel, along. But within weeks, a conflict on the other side of the country—the Civil War (1861–1865)—was to change Nevada's destiny.

War and Statehood

The Civil War, a conflict between Northern and Southern states, began on April 12, 1861. The Northern states were known as the Union (a term used then for the United States),

These tracks for the transcontinental railroad passed by the Humboldt River near Iron Point in the late 1860s.

and the eleven Southern states that seceded, or withdrew, from the Union were called the Confederacy. Many battles were fought, and more than six hundred thousand lives were lost. The major battles were fought thousands of miles away, but Nevada played an important role in the war. The Union used Comstock silver (silver from the Comstock Lode) to help pay for soldiers and supplies.

Some political leaders in Washington, DC, wanted to speed Nevada's entry into the Union. As a state, Nevada was likely to support the Union and the Republican Party. Congress passed an enabling act that set up an unusual procedure for Nevada statehood. This act involved the territorial government and the US president but not Congress. On October 31, 1864, Republican president Abraham Lincoln proclaimed Nevada the thirty-sixth state. The new state voted Republican in the US presidential election of 1864, just eight days after achieving statehood. In January 1865, Nevada's new member of the US House of Representatives voted in favor of the Thirteenth Amendment to the US Constitution. When it went into effect later in the year, the Thirteenth Amendment abolished (ended) slavery throughout the United States.

Nevada is sometimes called the Battle-Born State, because it achieved statehood during the Civil War. Nevada was not the only state to be admitted to the Union during the Civil War, however. West Virginia became the thirty-fifth state in 1863.

As the Civil War came to an end in 1865, Nevada continued to grow at a fast pace. The mines of Nevada were now producing silver worth an estimated $23 million every year. In 1869, the first transcontinental railroad, begun in 1863, was completed. The railroad passed through Nevada and connected Omaha, Nebraska, and the cities of the East with the fast-growing town of Sacramento, California. A cross-country trip that had once taken six difficult months could now be made in under a week. The railroad helped bring new residents to Nevada. It also helped to establish towns and cities along its route in different parts of Nevada, including Reno and Elko.

People kept coming to the state. Many were Americans from Midwestern or eastern states. Mark Twain wrote about the lure of quick riches in *Roughing It* in 1872.

"I would have been more or less than human if I had not gone mad like the rest. Cartloads of solid silver bricks, as large as pigs of lead, were arriving from the mills every day, and such sights as that gave substance to the wild talk about me. I succumbed and grew as frenzied as the craziest," he wrote.

People found other ways to make quick fortunes. In the early-morning hours of October 5, 1870, five masked men stopped a train outside Reno and rode off with a strongbox containing $50,000 worth of gold and silver. The raid is believed to be the first train robbery in the American West.

By the mid-1870s, nearly half of all Nevadans had been born outside the United States. Among them were Irish miners, German farmers, French-Canadian lumberjacks, Chinese railway workers, and Basque sheepherders (from the Basque region of northern Spain and southern France).

Through the late 1800s, Nevada was very important to the economy of the United States. The country's currency, or money, was based largely on the silver dollar. These dollars were minted from Nevada silver.

Boom and Bust

Nevada's history is like a roller-coaster ride—"boom" times of wealth and prosperity, followed by "busts" that bring hard times. The Comstock boom was

Paying the Soldiers

The gold and silver mines of Virginia City help finance the Union Army in the Civil War.

Las Vegas

Reno

1. Las Vegas: population 584,240

Las Vegas is known around the world for its glitzy resorts, shopping, restaurants, nightclubs, and casinos. Las Vegas was founded in 1911 and grew quickly when the state legalized gambling.

2. Henderson: population 275,354

Henderson is southeast of Las Vegas. It grew quickly in the 1940s, during World War II. Hoover Dam supplied cheap electricity to the factories that refined metals used to make warplanes and weapons.

3. Reno: population 226,012

Reno lies in a high valley formed by the Truckee River, at the base of the Sierra Nevada mountains along the border of California. Located on the California Trail, Reno grew from a small trading center to become "The Biggest Little City in the World."

4. Paradise: population 223,167

Paradise is a large city, but it is nearly unknown to visitors. Most of the casinos and hotels on the "Las Vegas Strip" are actually in Paradise, as are the area's international airport and the University of Nevada, Las Vegas.

5. North Las Vegas: population 216,700

North Las Vegas is located in the Mojave Desert, so its climate is mild in winter but very hot in summer. The temperature can easily reach 110°F (43°C), and when it does, the city sets up "cooling shelters" for the public.

6. Sunrise Manor: population 189,372

Sunrise Manor is not technically a city: It is a town governed by Clark County. It was formed in 1957 as a suburb of Las Vegas. Warm and dry in summer, it sometimes snows in winter.

7. Spring Valley: population 178,395

Spring Valley began as a housing development southwest of Las Vegas. When people flocked to the area, neighbors asked Clark County to form a town named Spring Valley. Spring Valley has grown from 1 square mile (2.6 sq km) to 33 square miles (85.5 sq km).

8. Enterprise: population 108,481

Enterprise, another suburban community near Las Vegas, has a town advisory board and is governed by Clark County. Many people moved to Enterprise to enjoy warm weather, golf, the nightlife of Las Vegas, and other recreation.

9. Sparks: population 90,258

Sparks was settled by European-Americans in the 1850s when the Southern Pacific Railroad gave each of its workers a house. Sparks is located near Reno and Pyramid Lake, and the Sierra Nevada range can be seen in the distance.

10. Carson City: population 55,274

Carson City, the capital, grew when the nearby Comstock Lode started a silver rush. The city borders Lake Tahoe, the Sierra Nevadas, and California.

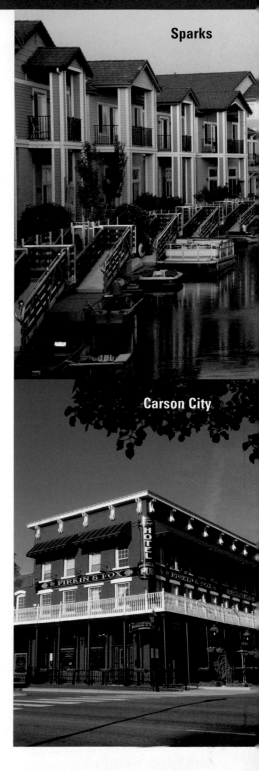

Sparks

Carson City

Belmont went from boom to bust, and now its abandoned buildings are in a historic district.

followed by the bust of the 1880s, when the US government began to switch the country's currency from silver to gold. Also, the silver in the Carson Valley finally began to run out.

The Nevada economy fell apart, and thousands of people left, in search of work in other parts of the country, such as California. The population of Nevada dropped from sixty-two thousand in 1880 to just forty-seven thousand in 1890. Many communities were simply abandoned. There are hundreds of ghost towns in Nevada—towns that were abandoned when gold or silver deposits ran out and miners left. For example, the population of Belmont, in Nye County, peaked at about four thousand in the mid-1870s. Today, it is a historic district with only a few residents.

Many Nevada ghost towns—such as Rhyolite and Goldfield, west of Las Vegas, and Chloride, near the Hoover Dam—are now tourist attractions.

The boom-and-bust cycle started up again in 1900, when Jim Butler, a rancher in central Nevada, went looking for a stray burro. He discovered a rich vein of silver. Within two years, a town called Tonopah had grown up around the discovery. The town had about three thousand residents. The mines of the Tonopah eventually produced silver valued at $125 million. But when the silver ran out, so did Tonopah's days as "Queen of the Silver Camps."

The Nevada mines that continued to produce were yielding incredible wealth, but most of the people who worked in them remained poor. In 1907, miners in the town of Goldfield, near Tonopah, grew angry over low pay and dangerous working conditions. They went on strike and refused to work in the mines until their lives were improved. The Goldfield strike, the most bitter labor conflict in the state's history, ended only when President Theodore Roosevelt sent in the US Army to prevent social warfare. The union was broken, and nonunion workers replaced the striking union workers.

Nevada is known as the boxing capital of the world, and the sport played a big role in the state's history. Informal bouts were common in the mining camps and in the towns that grew up around them. Nevada became the first state to legalize boxing in 1897. This was done so that a big-money heavyweight fight between Bob Fitzsimmons and Gentleman James Corbett could take place in Carson City. Thomas Edison filmed the bout, and the movie became the first feature film shown in the United States and the first big international film. It also gave exposure to the state. On July 9, 1910, Reno was the focus of national attention when Jack Johnson fought James Jeffries. Johnson was the first African-American heavyweight champion, and Jeffries was white. Bouts between the races were rare, and in some places illegal. In one of the biggest sporting events in history, Johnson won easily and earned $117,000, a huge amount at that time.

Fertile Fallon

The city of Fallon was awarded the nation's first "reclamation" project, a federal program that built dams to provide water to dryland farms. Fallon's dam, completed in 1915, created the "Oasis of Nevada." Today, Fallon continues to thrive and is also home to the US Navy's Fighter Weapons School, also known as "Top Gun" flight school.

Responses to the Great Depression

Nevada was hard hit by an economic downturn called the Great Depression. This economic collapse began in 1929 and caused widespread unemployment and poverty for many years. The federal government tried to create jobs by setting up new agencies, which employed people to carry out various useful projects, such as building roads, bridges, and airports.

One of these building projects, approved by Congress in 1928 but begun in 1931, was a huge dam across the Colorado River. Originally called the Boulder Dam, it was later renamed the Hoover Dam after the thirty-first US president, Herbert Hoover. The construction of the Hoover Dam

The Hoover Dam was near completion by 1935, four years after it was started.

took five years, five thousand workers, and more than 7 million tons (6.4 million metric tons) of concrete. An entire community, Boulder City, was built to house the workers and their families. The Hoover Dam project helped bring Nevada's economy back to life.

Another decision made in 1931 helped Nevada's economy. Lawmakers in the state decided to make gambling legal for the first time since 1910. Because gambling was against the law in most of the rest of the country, Nevada's new casinos soon became a popular attraction for out-of-state visitors with money to spend.

Nowhere did the changes have a greater impact than in the sleepy desert town known as Las Vegas, which is Spanish for "the meadows." The first casino in Las Vegas was built in 1931. But the city in those days was nothing like what it is today. Charles Miles, a resident of Las Vegas since 1932, remembered being a five-year-old in the city: "It was a little railroad town at that time—a place where everybody knew everybody and nobody ever locked their doors. It really was a great place to be a kid."

World War II (1939–1945), with its increased demand for metals, helped the Nevada economy rebound. The US government also established several military installations in the state during the war. The well-known Nellis Air Force Base, near Las Vegas, began as the Las Vegas Army Air Field in 1941.

Gaming Takes Hold

Few people saw the moneymaking potential of Las Vegas until Benjamin "Bugsy" Siegel, a gangster from New York City, opened the Flamingo Hotel and Casino in Las Vegas in 1946. The Flamingo eventually became a huge success, and in the years that followed, more casinos opened in Las Vegas.

In the late 1940s, Las Vegas hotel owners were looking for ways to keep customers gambling all night. They came upon the idea of chuck wagons, which were drawn out into the casinos at midnight, offering guests meals for a dollar. Eventually, the chuck wagons changed into inexpensive, all-you-can-eat buffets. Today, these buffets remain a part of the hotel-casino scene, although many are no longer so inexpensive.

The greatest stars of the entertainment world in the 1960s—from Frank Sinatra to Elvis Presley—came to Las Vegas to perform. These large-scale shows attracted even more people to the casinos and the gaming tables, bringing more money into Nevada.

Legalized gambling turned Nevada into a tourist destination. The Golden Nugget opened in 1946 in Las Vegas.

Much of the money was going into the wrong pockets, however. Criminal organizations owned or controlled many of the hotels and casinos in Las Vegas. By the late 1950s, the Nevada Gaming Commission was established to license and oversee gambling operations. In the early 1960s, the commission banned people with criminal records from entering or operating a casino, eventually separating crime from the casino operations.

The effort to rid Las Vegas of its criminal connections was supported in 1967, when the Nevada legislature passed the Corporate Gaming Act. This law made it possible for corporations to own casinos. In the end, the criminal organizations were unable to raise the enormous amount of money it cost to build new casino-hotels. By the early 1980s, corporations had taken over the running of Las Vegas resorts.

Nevada and Nuclear Testing

In 1951, the federal government began to test nuclear bombs in Nevada. The state was chosen because it had large tracts of land with almost no residents. The test area now known as the Nevada Test Site covers about 1,350 square miles (3,500 sq km) of desert. It is bigger than the entire state of Rhode Island. The site is just 65 miles (105 km) northwest of Las Vegas. The US government conducted hundreds of its nuclear weapons tests here.

In the early days, most Americans believed nuclear testing was necessary for the country's security. The Union of Soviet Socialist Republics (USSR) and other countries

Nevadans are concerned about the health effects of underground nuclear testing at Frenchman Flat at the Nevada Test Site.

Nevada State Highway 375, which passes near a military base called Area 51, is known as the ET Highway because of the many Unidentified Flying Objects reportedly seen from the road.

were developing nuclear weapons, and the United States wanted to be able to deter international war or defend itself during a nuclear attack. But many people were not aware of the long-term effects of radiation, which is given off during weapons tests. Radiation can cause many serious health problems, including cancer.

The US government conducted its first nuclear tests above the ground. Eventually, the government stopped this practice. The last atmospheric test occurred at the Nevada Test Site in 1962. Then, the government conducted tests underground. The last underground test took place in 1992.

Secret Site

The now-closed Wendover Air Force base near the Utah border was the secret site for pilots training to fly the *Enola Gay*, the airplane that dropped the atomic bomb on Nagasaki and Hiroshima, Japan, ending World War II.

Nevadans worry about the long-term impact of all those nuclear explosions on the environment and on their health. A great deal of radiation from the Nevada Test Site passed into the state's air, water, and soil. Many people point to high rates of serious illness—especially in the area downwind from the site—as the direct result of the nuclear radiation.

Nevada State Highway 375 runs for 98 miles (158 km) in south-central Nevada. In 1996, it was officially named the Extraterrestrial Highway because of the many Unidentified Flying Objects, or UFOs, reported on the road. It is true that the ET Highway passes near a US military base called Area 51, which seems to be used by the federal government for highly classified programs. Some people speculate that Area 51 holds alien spacecraft that crashed in the nearby desert, while others believe a lack of information encourages imaginations to run wild.

Call Me Lonely

The Nevada section of US-50, a transcontinental highway, is known as "The Loneliest Road in America." Eureka, a town on the highway, calls itself the "Loneliest Town on the Loneliest Road" and a sign on an emergency roadside telephone reads the "Loneliest Phone in America."

Modern Nevada

Nevadans still worry about their environment. Hundreds of thousands of people have poured into the state in the past half-century, seeking the good life that Nevada promised them and their families. And as they have arrived, they have changed the state and its environment.

The fast-growing population of Nevada required new housing, new roads, and new schools. Until the economic downturn that began in late 2007, many parts of the state were booming with construction. This was especially true in the area around Las Vegas, which was expanding several miles farther out into the desert every year as new housing developments were built. By 2011, however, average home prices in Nevada had fallen by 65 percent, and the state's unemployment rate had risen by more than 7 percentage points. It was one of the states hardest hit by the economic slump and housing bust.

Nevada has experienced many booms and busts, and there were indications by 2015 that the economy was improving again. Unemployment had dropped and home prices had rebounded. The state has always managed to protect its special way of life. Most Nevadans are confident that it will continue to be able to do so.

10 KEY DATES IN STATE HISTORY

1. 10,000 BCE–1150 CE

The earliest people live in what is now Nevada.

2. 1843-1844

John C. Frémont explores Nevada and publishes maps of the region. Settlers followed his trails, and steam locomotives loaded up on water from springs he mapped out.

3. 1857

The Comstock Lode, the richest silver deposit in the US, is discovered near Carson City on property partly owned by Henry Comstock. The official value of the gold and silver taken from the mine was $305,779,612.

4. October 31, 1864

Nevada becomes the thirty-sixth state. To achieve statehood quickly, citizens of the territory telegraphed the entire state constitution to President Lincoln, at a cost of $3,416.

5. November 3, 1914

Women gain the right to vote in Nevada, six years before women gain the right to vote nationally.

6. October 9, 1936

The Boulder Dam, renamed the Hoover Dam in 1947, starts sending electricity to Los Angeles. The dam, completed in 1935, stands 726 feet (221 m) above the canyon floor.

7. January 27, 1951

The US Atomic Energy Commission tests nuclear bombs above ground in the southern Nevada desert for the first time.

8. January 3, 2007

Nevadan Harry Reid, who was elected a US senator in 1987, becomes majority leader of the Senate.

9. Oct. 20, 2010

The Western Hemisphere's largest single-span concrete bridge, which towers 1,900 feet (579 m) over the Colorado River by the Hoover Dam, opens.

10. May 2015

Oak Ridge National Laboratory in Tennessee begins a test run of trucking radioactive uranium waste to a nuclear waste landfill at the Nevada National Security Site, north of Las Vegas.

People have been drawn to Nevada by places such as the Tahoe Rim Trail overlooking Lake Tahoe.

The People

For decades, Nevada has been one of the fastest-growing states in the country. In 1980, its population was about eight hundred thousand. By 2010, that number had increased to more than 2.7 million. The US census bureau estimates that by 2020, Nevada's population will be close to three million. Most of the state's new residents have settled in Clark County, the area that includes Las Vegas. The explosive growth in Nevada's population clearly shows that many are drawn to the state because of its varied landscapes, climate, and lifestyles. The new Nevadans have changed the Silver State in many ways, making it a more diverse place.

Hispanic Americans

Hispanic Americans have a long history in Nevada, which was part of Mexico before 1848. Mexican Americans were present when Las Vegas was founded in 1905. For many years, Hispanics were a small minority in Nevada. In recent years, however, Hispanic Americans have made up the fastest-growing segment of Nevada's population. The number of Hispanic residents grew from about 394,000 in 2000 to more than 716,000 in 2010. This represents an increase of almost 82 percent. More than one-quarter of Nevada's population is of Hispanic ancestry.

Most Hispanic Americans in Nevada trace their origins to Mexico. But as this group has increased in size, its diversity has increased as well. Today, the state's Hispanic-American population includes residents of Puerto Rican or Cuban ancestry, as well as many people who trace their origins to Central America or South America.

The Earliest Nevadans

Native Americans, who have been in the area for thousands of years, were the earliest Nevadans.

Eight petroglyph sites in Nevada are listed on the National Register of Historic Places. Some of these sites have hundreds of petroglyphs, many dating back about one thousand years. The descendants of the people who created these petroglyphs experienced a long, tragic decline after the arrival of white people. They are now one of the smallest— and poorest—minority groups in the state.

Members of the Paiute tribe wear traditional clothing to a powwow in Las Vegas.

Native Americans make up slightly more than one percent of Nevada's population. Many of them still live on reservations, such as the Duck Valley Indian Reservation, which covers almost 300,000 acres (120,000 ha) on the Nevada-Idaho border and is home to more than 2,300 Paiute and Shoshone.

In recent years, Nevada's Native Americans have successfully argued court cases to take back land they believe was unfairly taken from them—or at least receive payment for that land. The Native Americans of Nevada have used settlement payments to build new businesses, such as golf courses and resorts, which bring in money and create jobs. Others own cattle ranches and mining operations. Perhaps most important, these groups have worked hard to keep their cultures alive, through museums and festivals such as powwows, which are Native American gatherings that include music, dancing, and storytelling.

The Native Americans of Nevada are very active in government and in protecting and preserving the land. The Pyramid Lake Paiute Tribe Museum in Nixon details the tribe's long history with the lake, the fish, and wildlife. The tribe oversees a national bird sanctuary and operates a fish hatchery. The Washoe tribe plays an important role in protecting endangered habitats around Lake Tahoe. With the tribe's longstanding knowledge of the area's plants and animals, tribal experts contribute to Nevada's land resource management programs. Many members of the Western Shoshone tribe are active in conservation programs such as water use and recycling.

African Americans

African Americans, too, have a long history in Nevada. In 1850, James Pierson Beckwourth, a mountain man born into slavery in Virginia, discovered an important route for wagon trains through the Sierra Nevada to California. This path is known as the Beckwourth Trail. Benjamin Palmer, another former slave, is believed to have been the first African-American settler in Nevada. He built a 400-acre (160 ha) ranch near Sheridan in 1853, and he worked it for more than forty years. Near the end of the Civil War, President Lincoln was up for re-election. Those who were anti-slavery feared that the Democrats would win and slavery would continue. In an important Republican rally in Virginia City, African-American Thomas R. Street, of Comstock, delivered an impassioned speech by reading the Emancipation Proclamation and urging people to vote for President Lincoln. His words were published in newspapers throughout the West.

Natural Heat

Nevada has 321 hot springs, more than any other state. Some of the hottest are nearly 200°F [95°C]. Today, many people heat their homes with hot water piped up from the earth while others enjoy a hardy and healthy soak.

Today, African Americans make up more than 8 percent of the Silver State's population.

The Basques

The Basques are a prominent ethnic group in Nevada. Most Basque Nevadans have ancestors who came to the state from Spain. Many Basques saw a resemblance between northern Nevada and their homes in the Pyrenees

Andre Agassi

Tony Hsieh

DeMarco Murray

1. Andre Agassi

Andre Agassi, born in Las Vegas in 1970, was taught to play tennis by his Armenian father. Agassi won all four Grand Slam events and an Olympic gold medal. In 2011, Agassi was inducted into the International Tennis Hall of Fame.

2. Charlotte Hunter Arley

Charlotte Hunter Arley began practicing law in Reno in 1947. There were only three female lawyers in Nevada at the time. In her first trial before the state Supreme Court, the opposing attorney was also a woman. She won and enjoyed a long, successful career.

3. Dat-So-La-Lee

Dat-So-La-Lee was born near Sheridan in 1844. A member of the Washoe, she was a cleaning woman who developed a basket-weaving style that mixed traditional and modern designs. Her work is on display in the Smithsonian Institution.

4. Tony Hsieh

Tony Hsieh is the head of Zappos, one of the most successful online businesses in the world. He has invested in a blighted area of downtown Las Vegas and lured many new companies to move there.

5. DeMarco Murray

DeMarco Murray played high school football in Las Vegas and went on to become a star National Football League running back with the Dallas Cowboys and the Philadelphia Eagles. He runs the DeMarco Murray Foundation, which gives back-to-school supplies to many low-income students.

6. Howard Hughes

Howard Hughes was a brilliant and eccentric billionaire who was a pilot, movie producer, and businessman. He was awarded a Congressional Medal of Honor. In 1966, he bought six Las Vegas casinos and forced criminal activity out of Las Vegas.

7. Anne Martin

Born in Empire in 1875, Anne Martin taught at Nevada State University and became involved in the women's suffrage movement. She helped Nevada's women to receive the right to vote in 1914.

8. Sarah Winnemucca

Sarah Winnemucca, a Paiute princess born in 1844, worked to improve the lives of her tribe, established schools, and fought for Native American rights. Her 1883 autobiography, *Life Among the Paiutes: Their Wrongs and Claims*, is a classic.

9. Wovoka

Wovoka, a Paiute holy man, urged Native Americans to perform the Ghost Dance, which he said would expel white people. The Ghost Dance terrified white society and led to the 1890 Massacre at Wounded Knee, where two hundred Lakota Sioux were killed by US soldiers.

10. Steve Wynn

Steve Wynn, born in Connecticut in 1942, left college to take over the family bingo operation. He moved to Las Vegas in 1967 and upgraded hotels and casinos. In 1998, Wynn opened a $1.6 billion resort with a museum-quality art collection.

Sarah Winnemucca

Wovoka

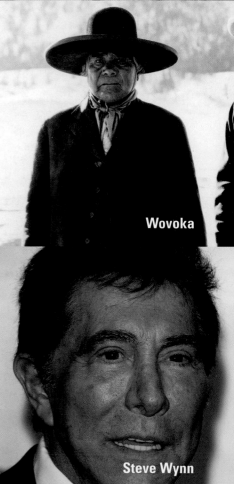
Steve Wynn

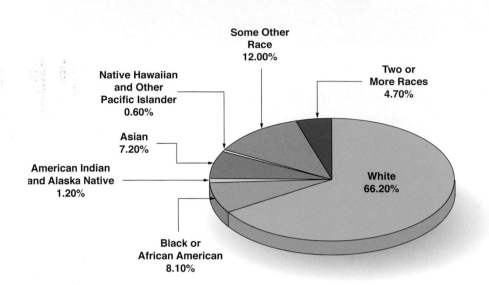

**Total Population
2,700,551**

Hispanic or Latino (of any race):
• **716,501 people (26.5%)**

Note: The pie chart shows the racial breakdown of the state's population based on the categories used by the US Bureau of the Census. The Census Bureau reports information for Hispanics or Latinos separately, since they may be of any race. Percentages in the pie chart may not add to 100 because of rounding.

Source: US Bureau of the Census, 2010 Census

Some Other Race 12.00%

Two or More Races 4.70%

Native Hawaiian and Other Pacific Islander 0.60%

Asian 7.20%

American Indian and Alaska Native 1.20%

White 66.20%

Black or African American 8.10%

Mountains region, on the border between Spain and France. When they arrived, many settled in the northern part of the state around Reno, Elko, and Winnemucca. Many took up their traditional occupations, becoming sheepherders and, eventually, successful sheep ranchers.

In 1873, a Basque immigrant named Pedro Altube founded the Spanish Ranch, a huge cattle operation in the Independence Valley. He brought so many of his friends and relatives to America that he is known as the Father of the Basques in the West.

Modern Basques in Nevada have also built many hotels. One of the great pleasures of a drive across Nevada today is stopping at a small-town hotel for a Basque meal. This meal could include traditional foods such as the spiced-pork sausage called chorizo, garbanzo beans, and grilled lamb.

The Basque culture is very old and distinct, and the Basque language is believed to be unrelated to any other language in the world. Like other cultural groups, the state's Basques have their own traditions and festivals, such as the annual National Basque Festival in Elko.

Asian Americans

Many people of Asian origin or descent have also come to Nevada. Some are Asian Americans who have moved from other states. Others are recent immigrants from such countries as India, China, Japan, and the Philippines. Some Asian Nevadans are descendants of the Chinese who came to the region more than one hundred years ago. Most of those early immigrants came to work on the transcontinental and other railroads. They faced terrible discrimination. Yet in the 1850s, many Chinese miners settled in western Nevada. Despite laws made by the Gold Hill Mining District that forbade Chinese people from owning a mining claim, the Chinese became successful by turning to other occupations, such as owning restaurants, hotels, and laundry businesses. In other mining regions, Chinese miners, supported by wealthy Chinese in San Francisco, bought up old and abandoned claims from European-Americans and made them successful, especially in Elko County and Winnemucca. Throughout the mining boom, the Chinese miners had friendly relationships with the Native Americans and the European-Americans of the area. Today, many Asian Americans have thriving businesses and host various cultural festivals.

Education

Nevada has a long history of educating its young citizens, for better or for worse. Eliza Mott of Carson Valley started the first school. In 1852, she opened a school in her farmhouse kitchen. Twenty students, aged five to eleven, shared three textbooks—a reader, a spelling book, and an arithmetic book. In 1876, Virginia City built an elegant and modern (for that time) school. It was designed to hold more than one thousand students

The Chinese New Year is celebrated each year in a big way in Las Vegas.

and was one of the first such buildings to have drinking fountains and flush toilets. In 1878, the school, known as the Fourth Ward, was the first Nevada school to award diplomas to students successfully completing nine grades. In 1909, the Fourth Ward School included all twelve grades. In 1884, Sarah Winnemucca established Nevada's first school for Native Americans, called Peabody's Institute, near Lovelock.

In 1890, the state of Nevada established the Stewart Indian School, a federal boarding school for Native Americans. There were several such schools in the West, and the Stewart School, named after a Nevada senator, was the only school of its kind in Nevada. Children from the Walapai, Paiute, Washoe, and Shoshone, as well as children from tribes outside of Nevada, were forced to leave their homes and families and learn the "ways of the white man." The school was very strict. They forbade students to speak their native language and refused any practice of students' native culture and religion. Upon arrival, students were bathed in kerosene, and their long hair was cut. They were each given "American" names and were forced to wear "white man's" clothing. Students were taught basic education and trades such as carpentry. After graduating from the school, many students went back to their families and could not communicate with them. They had forgotten how to speak their own language. One former student recalls that his grandmother simply said, "Who are you?" The Stewart

The University of Nevada, Las Vegas educates more than thirty thousand students, the second-highest number in the state.

Indian School operated until 1980. Today the school, its eighty-three buildings, and its 109-acre (44.1 ha) campus are maintained by the US National Park Service.

Today, Nevada, like other states, strives to find creative ways to provide good public education. Urban schools are overcrowded. Rural schools are very expensive to operate. To save money, Nevada has merged many rural schools. As a consequence, some students undergo two- to three-hour bus rides each day. In 2015, the state legislature gave each student an education account that could be used to pay for supplies, transportation, or partial tuition in charter schools or private schools. Time will tell, as many people believe that students in poorer neighborhoods will not fare as well as students in wealthier communities.

The oldest college in the state is the University of Nevada, Reno, which was founded in 1874 in Elko. The state's largest public university today is the University of Nevada, Las Vegas. Additionally there are five public two-year colleges, five private colleges, including a regional health sciences college, and several technical and vocational schools.

A Place of Opportunities

Most people who have moved to Nevada from different states or countries came to Nevada to work, and work hard. The United States military established bases in Nevada, and over the years countless military personnel and their families have been transferred to Nevada. Many chose to stay. Some people have been drawn to the fast-paced life of Las Vegas. Others like the slower pace of the state's small towns and suburbs, while others embrace the wide-open spaces.

Many of the people who come to live in Nevada today are retired. Nevada has one of the largest populations of retirees who come from all over the country, lured by the many recreational activities, the low cost of living, and, of course, the warm, sunny weather. Many live in retirement communities.

The many changes in Nevada in recent years have made it a fascinating and complicated place. The modern world is very closely linked to the natural environment. Even the glittering hotels and casinos of Las Vegas and Reno are just a few minutes away from the natural beauty of the desert and the mountains. Many Nevadans, in fact, barely notice the neon-lit attractions that draw tourists. Some prefer hiking in the desert, visiting a museum, or enjoying local festivals.

In many ways, the people of Nevada have the best of all worlds. They treasure their pioneer heritage and the untouched beauty of the wilderness. At the same time, they are proud of the rapid pace of progress in the Silver State. Most Nevadans share great confidence in their state and hope that its future will be as exciting as its past.

10 KEY EVENTS ★ ★

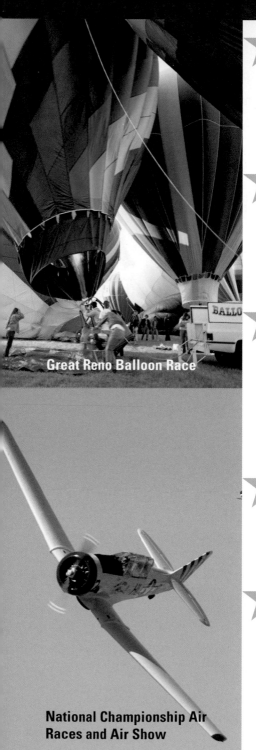

Great Reno Balloon Race

National Championship Air Races and Air Show

1. Great Reno Balloon Race

In early September, the blue skies above Reno fill with hot air balloons for the Great Reno Balloon Race. More than a hundred balloons participate in this three-day event, which attracts an average of 150,000 people.

2. Hispanic International Day Parade and Festival

On the second Saturday of every October, Henderson hosts this family-oriented cultural parade followed by a music festival. The local Hispanic community shares new and traditional music, food, and art from various countries.

3. Jim Butler Days

Once a year—every Memorial Day weekend—Tonopah remembers the man who went looking for a lost burro and started the last great Nevada mining rush. Activities include a parade, a street dance, and contests in timber tossing and spike driving.

4. National Basque Festival

The Basques of Nevada say *"Ongi etorri"* ("Welcome") at this grand celebration of their traditional culture, every July in Elko.

5. National Championship Air Races and Air Show

Every September, the skies above Reno roar with the sounds of different kinds of aircraft, from World War II fighters to racing jets. There are five days of racing and six classes of aircraft, with speeds exceeding 500 miles (800 km) per hour.

6. National Cowboy Poetry Gathering

At the end of every January, Elko celebrates its Old West heritage. That means big hats, big boots, big stories (some folks might even call them tall tales), and, of course, poetry.

7. National Finals Rodeo

For one week in December, Las Vegas becomes the Cowboy Capital of the World. This event—with bareback riding, calf roping, and barrel racing—is the most important competition on the rodeo circuit.

8. Nevada Day Celebration

Carson City celebrates the day Nevada became a state—October 31, 1864—with a parade and other festivities. Many events, such as the World Championship Rock Drilling Contest, recall the state's mining past.

9. Spirit of Wovoka Days

Every August, the town of Yerington, on the Walker River, celebrates the legacy of Wovoka, the Paiute mystic and founder of the Ghost Dance Movement. Among the highlights of this powwow are traditional shawl and bustle dances by various Native American groups.

10. Virginia City Camel Races

This event, held in Virginia City each September, looks back at a time when camels carried freight to and from the mines of the Comstock Lode. In addition to camels, ostriches and emus are featured. The event takes place at the top of a historic mining quarry.

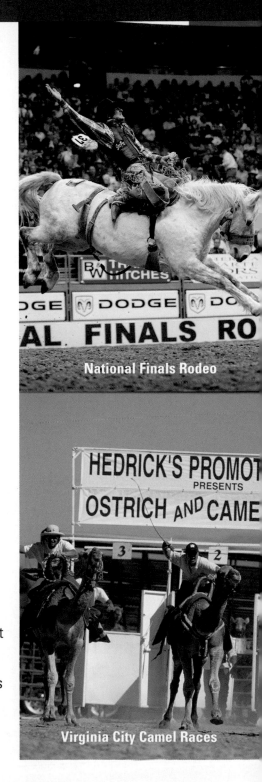

National Finals Rodeo

Virginia City Camel Races

Citizens have had a great effect on government actions in Nevada by protesting nuclear testing and waste storage and other activities.

How the Government Works

The people of Nevada are represented by three levels of government: local, state, and federal. Each of these levels is, in its own way, extremely important to the running of the state.

The state's cities, towns, and villages have their own local governments. Most have mayors and city or town councils, elected by local voters every two years. Mayors and councils make decisions about property taxes, schools, and other local issues. Nevada is also divided into seventeen counties, managed by boards of commissioners that are elected every two years. One example of a county government's responsibilities is maintaining police departments.

Nevada's Native American reservations have their own governments. The residents choose their leaders, who are responsible for the police and fire departments, road repairs, and other important services within the reservations.

Nevada's Government

Nevada's state government, which makes decisions that affect the entire state, is based on a system of checks and balances. This means that the three separate branches, or parts,

Historical exhibits and the governor's office can be found inside the state capitol.

of the state government—the executive, legislative, and judicial branches—work together and no branch can become too powerful.

Executive

The executive branch, headed by the governor, handles the day-to-day management of the state and makes sure that Nevada's laws and regulations are properly enforced. The governor and the other senior officials of the executive branch— the lieutenant governor, secretary of state, attorney general, treasurer, and controller—are elected by the state's voters. These officials serve four-year terms and cannot hold office for more than two terms.

Legislative

The legislative branch creates new state laws and makes changes to existing laws. The Nevada legislature has two chambers, or houses: the forty-two-member assembly and the twenty-one-member senate. Members of the assembly serve two-year terms, while members of the senate serve for four years. Both are elected by the voters of their individual state electoral districts. Legislators may not seek election to a house in which they have served twelve years or more.

Judicial

The judicial branch—the court system—makes sure that Nevada's laws are properly interpreted and enforced. The highest level of the judicial branch, the state Supreme Court, hears appeals from the lower courts and decides whether new laws agree with Nevada's constitution. The Supreme Court has a chief justice and six associate justices, who are elected for six-year terms. Sixty district court justices, who also serve six-year terms, hear important criminal and civil cases. Sixty-four justices sit in the justice courts, which preside over the preliminary phases of important criminal and civil cases. Municipal courts handle less serious cases. The district courts also act as appeal courts for cases from justice and municipal courts.

How a Bill Becomes a Law

The governor, local government officials, organizations, and citizens often ask the members of the Nevada state assembly and senate to pass new laws or change existing ones. When a lawmaker agrees with a suggestion, he or she proposes a new law—called a bill—and a legislative attorney prepares a draft version of the bill. Then a committee from the house where the bill has arisen considers the draft bill. Most of these committees have a special focus, such as education, taxes, or agriculture. Committee members discuss the details of the bill. They usually make changes, called amendments. If they support the bill, they present it to the house, which debates and then votes on it.

The state capitol in Carson City was completed in 1871.

If the house where the bill originates approves, or passes, the draft bill, it goes to the other house, where the process begins again. If the houses pass a different version of the bill, the bill is sent to a joint conference committee. This committee, which includes representatives from both houses, tries to create a compromise version of the bill. This new bill is then presented to both houses for a vote. It must be passed first by the house in which it started.

To become law, a bill must be approved in a vote by a majority of the members of both houses. This requires twenty-two votes in the assembly and eleven votes in the senate. Bills with tax or fee increases require a two-thirds majority in each house to pass. Once the bill has been approved, it is sent to the governor, who either signs it, making it a law, or vetoes—rejects—it. The legislature can override the governor's veto, by giving the bill a two-thirds majority vote in each house. If that happens, the bill becomes law even though the governor rejected it.

Citizen Power

The citizens of Nevada can suggest or reject laws, using the power of "**initiative** and **referendum**." In an initiative, voters suggest a law. If enough voters agree with the proposal, the initiative is put on the ballot during an election. In a referendum, voters can repeal an existing law. When the state legislature is in session, citizens can watch debates and sit in on committee meetings. Nevada state legislators officially convene, or meet, every two years. However, they can meet in special sessions.

The Federal Government

Nevada is also represented in the US Congress in Washington, DC. The state's voters elect two senators, like all states, and four members of the House of Representatives. Nevada gained the fourth representative in 2013, because of its large population increase, as recorded in the 2010 Census. Representation at the federal level is especially important in Nevada, because the federal government is unusually powerful in the state.

The US government owns or controls more than 87 percent of the land in Nevada, in the form of military bases, national parks, and other holdings. There is sometimes conflict between Nevadans and the federal government. A rancher who wants to herd cattle on a particular piece of land may have to deal with many different federal agencies, such as the Bureau of Land Management, the Fish and Wildlife Service, the Forest Service, and even the military.

One type of government activity probably troubles many Nevadans more than any other: the past use of the desert as a place to test nuclear weapons and its potential future use as a site to

Silly Laws

Reno likes to keep citizens on their toes. Section 8 of the city code makes it illegal to sit or lie down on public sidewalks. It is also illegal to put a bench, chair, stool, or blanket on any street, alley, or sidewalk, without permission from the city council.

Bob Fulkerson, an environmental activist in Nevada, led a protest in Reno against the Yucca Mountain nuclear waste project.

store nuclear waste materials. Nevadans' nuclear concerns became even more serious in 1987, when the federal government announced plans to create a huge storage area for nuclear waste at Yucca Mountain, at the edge of the Nevada Test Site. The plan called for 77,000 tons (69,854 t) of radioactive material—such as spent fuel from nuclear power plants—to be stored at Yucca Mountain. The project required that metal containers for the waste be able to contain radiation for ten thousand years, yet as detractors say, there is no way to test the material.

Despite years of government assurances that Yucca Mountain would be safe, a majority of Nevadans—more than 70 percent, according to some opinion polls—opposed the plan. Although a plan to go ahead with the Yucca Mountain project had been approved earlier, President Barack Obama halted work on the project in 2009. In 2010, he appointed the Blue Ribbon Commission on America's Nuclear Future to recommend a long-term solution for disposing of nuclear waste in the United States. In 2012, the commission released its recommendations. The first of these was that a consent-based approach should be used to select sites for nuclear waste facilities. The commission simply said that if the local people opposed a project, it would not succeed. The statement was a victory for Nevadans who had opposed the Yucca Mountain project. However, the actual location of a nuclear waste storage facility remained to be determined. The controversy continued into 2015 when Republican governor Brian Sandoval declared that Yucca Mountain would never be safe enough.

POLITICAL FIGURES

FROM NEVADA

Sadie Dotson Hurst: State Legislator, 1918-1920

Sadie Dotson Hurst moved to Reno as a mother and a widow. She quickly got involved in the drive for women's voting rights. In 1918, four years after Nevada women won the right to vote, voters in Washoe County elected her as their first female legislator.

Harry Reid: United States Senator, 1987-2017

Harry Reid was born in 1939 in Searchlight, Nevada. As a US senator representing the people of Nevada, he held office from 1987 to 2015; as of the writing of this book, he announced that he would not choose to run for reelection in 2016 and would end his senatorial career in 2017. In 2007, Senator Reid became the Senate majority leader.

Brian Sandoval: Governor, 2010-

Brian Sandoval became the first Hispanic in Nevada to hold statewide office. He served as the Nevada attorney general from 2005 to 2009 and was appointed to a United States District Court judgeship by a unanimous vote of the US Senate. In 2010, he was elected the Republican governor of Nevada.

NEVADA
YOU CAN MAKE A DIFFERENCE

Contacting Lawmakers

All citizens can contact the government officials who represent them to express their views about proposed legislation and other issues.

To contact the governor, go to **gov.nv.gov**
Click on Contact on the menu bar. Then click on the link named Email the Governor to send the governor an email message.

To contact your state legislators, go to **www.leg.state.nv.us**
To find your assembly member or your state senator, click on Members and then Assembly Members; each member has an email address listed.

To contact your representatives in the US Congress, go to **www.congress.org**
Enter your zip code to find your representatives.

Wild Horses

Wild horses may run free in Nevada today, but in earlier times they were sometimes rounded up, captured using airplanes, packed into trucks, and sent to slaughterhouses to be made into pet food. One day, a woman from Reno named Velma Bronn witnessed a baby horse being trampled by other horses who were packed tightly into a truck headed for the slaughterhouse. The cruelty overwhelmed her. She herself had experienced cruelty, after contracting polio as a child and being taunted by children for her atrophied legs. So she went to work writing letters and campaigning for better treatment for the wild horses. She earned the nickname "Wild Horse Annie." Eventually, a state law was passed banning wild horse hunting by airplanes and land vehicles. Yet the pet food companies found ways around the law. Bronn went back to the campaign trail and enlisted school children to write letters to their members of Congress asking for protection for the wild horses. Bronn went to Washington, DC, and testified before Congress, asking for an end to the capture of wild horses. Through her hard work and persistence and with the enormous help of school children and other concerned Nevadans, President Richard Nixon signed the Wild Free-Roaming Horse and Burro Act in 1971, giving wild horses and burros protection on federal land.

Facilities such as the Spring Valley Wind Farm make Nevada a leader in the use of renewable energy.

Making
a Living

Nevada residents make their living in many different ways, both old and new. A Nevada worker might be a card dealer in a casino, a cowboy in Elko, a teacher, shop owner, or nurse in any community in the state. Nevada's economy needs all these types of workers—and many more.

From the Land

Mining remains an important industry. More than 2,300 businesses are connected to the mining industry. Open-pit and underground mines yield gold, silver, and semi-precious gemstones, such as turquoise and opals, including the very rare cat's eye and black fire opals. Nevada's land also produces construction materials, including gypsum, limestone, and clays. Nevada leads the nation in the production of gold. New technologies, such as satellite imaging to locate deposits and remote controlled digging equipment, make mining safer and more efficient. Today's mining does not require the backbreaking work it did in the 1800s. The new digging equipment and other advances in technology have replaced the miners who used to go into dangerous underground areas. This has reduced the number of workers in Nevada's mines, but a job in a mine pays about double the wage of the average worker.

Nevada produces more gold by far than any other state.

In Silver Peak, the Rockwood lithium mine is the only lithium mine in the United States. Lithium is one of the Earth's oldest metals, used in medicines and glass making, and today it is the basis for the most advanced batteries that are used in computers, cell phones, and electric cars. The electric car company, Tesla, is building a major highway between its lithium-ion battery factory in northern Nevada and the Rockwood lithium mine.

Nevada is not a big oil-producing state, but oil companies are now investigating oil and natural gas reserves that were previously too difficult to reach. There are test sites near Elko and permits to explore for oil on 174,000 acres (70,415 ha) of government land. If enough oil is found, companies plan to extract oil by fracking. This is a process using pressurized water and chemicals to break up deep underground rock formations that contain pockets of natural gas and oil. Many oppose fracking. They fear it will contaminate precious water resources. However, others believe fracking would provide jobs and help the nation become more energy independent.

Agriculture has always been difficult in Nevada and now represents a very small part of the state's economy. Cattle and sheep ranches are the main source of agricultural income. Their meat and wool are shipped all over the world. Horse ranches and dairy and poultry farms are found throughout western and southeastern Nevada. Farmers grow potatoes, onions, and livestock feed, such as barley, alfalfa, and hay. Alfalfa is a leading crop in the state, and alfalfa hay is sold to dairy farms in surrounding states. Alfalfa cubes and compressed bales are also exported overseas. Alfalfa seeds are another substantial crop.

A young boy herds cattle near Baker. Cattle are one of the leading sources of agricultural income in the state.

The Newlands Project—the first **irrigation** project ever built by the US government—diverted the waters of the Carson and Truckee Rivers to the Lahontan Valley. The 1903 to 1908 project brought water, and farming, to an 87,000-acre (35,000 ha) stretch of desert through a long series of canals, dams, and irrigation ditches. The project continues to operate today. In irrigated and water conservation areas, such as farms near Pyramid Lake, farmers grow crops that would not ordinarily grow in such a dry climate, such as tomatoes and grapes. Farmers and ranchers sell many of the state's agricultural products locally but also export products to other states and countries. Although agriculture is a small part of the state's economy, it is still worth more than $500 million every year.

Other Industries

Other industries continue to grow in Nevada. Manufacturing is becoming a more important segment of the state's economy, especially in Reno, Henderson, and North Las Vegas. Manufacturing production includes food and beverage products, computers, electronics, and plastic and rubber products. In 2014, Nevada's factories exported nearly $7 billion of goods. Eighty-five percent of all goods made and sold are by small businesses. New businesses are attracted to Nevada's skilled workers, low costs, and low taxes. Nevadans pay less tax than the residents of almost any other state. Zappos, a successful online company in Las Vegas that sells shoes and clothes, generates more than $2 billion

Gaming

Gold

1. Agriculture

Most Nevada agriculture is in livestock production, such as cattle, sheep, and poultry. Nevada ranches rank third in the nation in size, averaging 3,500 acres (1,416 ha).

2. Gaming

Half of Nevada's economy is based on gaming. Huge corporations such as Bally, Harrah's, and Wynn Resorts operate casinos in the state. Gaming machine manufacturers, such as International Game Technology and Boyd Gaming, are also a major source of income.

3. Gold

Nevada's early economy was built on silver mining, but today, gold is an even more important resource. The state is the third-richest source of gold in the world, after South Africa and Australia.

4. Information Technology

Information technology is one of the fastest growing industries in the state. As of 2015, the world's largest and most powerful data storage facility was being built near Reno, where Apple Computers has a large and growing iCloud storage center.

5. Manufacturing

Nevada's manufacturing sector is concentrated mostly around Reno and the Las Vegas suburbs of Henderson and North Las Vegas. Nevada's manufacturers produce industrial machinery, computer software, food products, chemicals, and printing products.

NEVADA ★ ★ ★ ★ ★

Tourism

Water Power

6. Military

Nearly twenty thousand people, soldiers and civilians, are employed on military bases in Nevada. There are two Air Force bases, one naval air station, and a large Army weapons depot.

7. Renewable Energy

Nevada is eighth among states in the percentage of energy produced by renewable sources. Facilities include the Spring Valley wind farm in Ely, large solar panel arrays in many locations, a biofuel refinery to convert waste to electricity in Reno, and **geothermal** energy.

8. Tourism

Tourism is by far Nevada's most important industry. Outdoor activities are popular attractions. The cities are, too—Las Vegas alone welcomed more than thirty-seven million visitors in 2010. These visitors spent almost $37 billion.

9. Transportation

A superb road, rail, and air transportation system keeps people and goods moving in and out of Nevada. Las Vegas's McCarran International Airport handles more than forty million passengers every year.

10. Water Power

Even though it is the driest state in the country, Nevada actually sends water to other places. Lake Mead provides water to millions of Nevadans and Californians. Turbines at the Hoover Dam also turn the power of rushing water into electricity.

Recipe for Gold Hill Rock Cookies

This Nevada roadhouse restaurant's recipe is a sweet, hearty, and tasty treat.

What You Need

Two eggs

1½ tablespoons (22 milliliters) warm water

One stick butter

¾ cup (177 mL) brown sugar

½ pound (227 grams) walnuts or pecans

½ pound (227 g) raisins

1¼ cups (296 mL) flour

¼ tablespoon (4 mL) salt

¼ tablespoon (4 mL) cinnamon

½ teaspoon (2.5 mL) baking soda

Two mixing bowls

Mixing spoon

Cookie sheets

Measuring cups and spoons

1 to 2 tablespoons (14 to 28 mL) of oil to grease cookie sheets

What To Do

- Pre-heat oven to 350°F (177°C).
- Mix butter and sugar until creamy. Add eggs and beat.
- In another bowl, mix flour, salt, and cinnamon.
- Dissolve the baking soda into the warm water.
- Add to butter, sugar, and egg mixture.
- Then add dry mixture to butter, sugar, and egg mixture. Beat slowly until ingredients are just blended.
- Fold in nuts and raisins.
- Drop by the teaspoonful onto oiled cookie sheets and bake until lightly browned.
- Have an adult help to remove hot cookie sheets from oven.
- Cool on cooling rack.
- See if you can try to eat just one!

Zappos, which has its headquarters in Las Vegas, generates billions of dollars in sales each year.

in sales each year. New technology start-up companies are also lured to Las Vegas, such as a company that invented and sells robots that are operated by iPhones.

Nevada's central position in the western United States makes it an important transportation hub. There are two international airports and two freight railroads. Trucking and warehousing are also flourishing.

More than 50 percent of Nevada's workers are employed in service industries. Service workers do something for others, rather than make a product. Lawyers, bankers, teachers, health care workers, and tradespeople are service workers. Most service workers in Nevada are employed in hotels, restaurants, casinos, and resorts.

Renewable Energy

With its wide-open, windy plains and its nearly relentless sunshine, Nevada is an ideal location for renewable energy projects. Many companies have moved into the state and built wind farms and solar panel arrays that deliver electricity. The Spring Valley wind farm in Ely generates 150 megawatts of power. There are four major solar power-generating arrays. One has more than one million solar panels on 450 acres (150 ha). Other renewable projects are a refinery that makes fuel from waste, and many geothermal power plants that use hot water and steam from hot springs to run electric turbines.

The Military

Nevada is home to Nellis Air Force Base, Creech Air Force Base, Fallon Naval Air Station, and Hawthorne Army Depot. Nellis has more squadrons than any other base, which includes a weapons school. Fallon has a naval weapons school, the Top Gun pilot program, and Navy SEAL combat training. Nevada, with its open spaces and empty landscape, is especially suitable for training operations, test piloting, military vehicle combat practice, drones development, and weapons testing. Nevada was the first state to issue driverless vehicle test licenses for military use. The Hawthorne Army Depot stores **munitions** on 145,000 acres (58,679 ha).

Information Technology

Information technology and online businesses are one of the fastest growing industries in the state. As of 2015, Nevada is home to the world's largest and most powerful data storage facility. Apple Computers has a large and growing iCloud storage center near Reno. Zappos has its headquarters and warehouses in Nevada, and Amazon.com also has warehouses in the state.

Tourism

The most important sector of Nevada's economy is tourism. In 2014, forty-one million tourists came to Nevada. This industry brings in more than half of the state's income, just as it has for more than half a century. While many parts of Nevada are ideal for tourists, Las Vegas tends to be the most popular. The city has more hotel rooms than anywhere else in the world. Many of the hotels and resorts in Las Vegas are inspired by certain themes, such as foreign countries and world landmarks—Egyptian pyramids or tropical islands.

Over the past few decades, the state has become a great place for family vacations. There are many shows, concerts, and other forms of entertainment for the whole family to enjoy. Nevada has many resorts, spas, amusement parks, swimming pools, and golf courses that offer fun, relaxing pastimes. Many conventions are also held in Las Vegas.

Great Basin National Park, created in 1986, is the only US national park located entirely in Nevada. Visitors climb mountains, such as Wheeler Peak. They

Rich Deposits

There are more turquoise mines in Nevada than all the rest of the states combined. The mines have generated millions of dollars since the early commercial mining days.

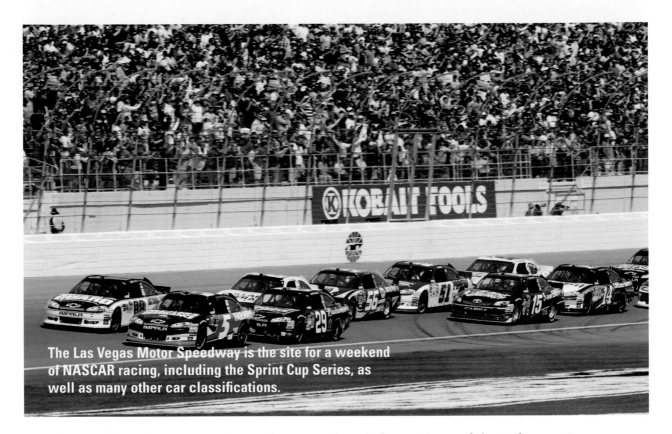

The Las Vegas Motor Speedway is the site for a weekend of NASCAR racing, including the Sprint Cup Series, as well as many other car classifications.

can also explore the spectacular underground rock formations of the Lehman Caves and walk on a glacier. Numerous state parks offer outdoor experiences such as water recreation activities at Lake Tahoe, Pyramid Lake, and Lake Mead, hikes in Echo Canyon, and climbing around the otherworldly red rock formations at Valley of Fire State Park. Tourists are also drawn to remote ghost towns and historic places that preserve the days of pioneers and mining booms. Amateur gold prospectors and rock hounds looking for opals, jasper, turquoise, topaz, and garnets, flock to the state, hoping to find small treasure while hiking and camping.

As of 2015, Nevada had no major league professional sports teams, but citizens root for many college sports teams and the Las Vegas 51s baseball team, which plays in the Triple-A level Pacific Coast League. Major golf tournaments, boxing matches, and rodeos are held in Las Vegas. The Las Vegas Motor Speedway is renowned for its National Association for Stock Car Auto Racing (NASCAR) events.

Workers are probably Nevada's most important resource. Their determination, drive, and energy show the same spirit as in the state's early days. While modern Nevadans are more likely to work for a resort hotel or a software company than at a silver mine or a cattle ranch, they continue to show a pioneering spirit. The people of Nevada are the main reason so many visitors come to the Silver State—and will keep coming for many years.

NEVADA
STATE MAP

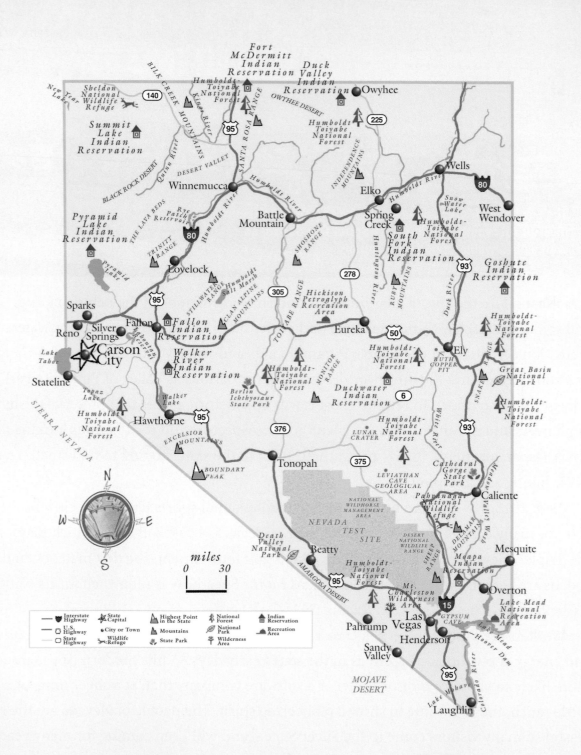

Fort McDermitt Indian Reservation
Duck Valley Indian Reservation
Sheldon National Wildlife Refuge
Summit Lake Indian Reservation
Humboldt-Toiyabe National Forest
OWYHEE DESERT
Owyhee
225
140
BILK CREEK MOUNTAINS
Kings River
95
SANTA ROSA RANGE
Humboldt River
DESERT VALLEY
Winnemucca
Battle Mountain
Humboldt-Toiyabe National Forest
INDEPENDENCE MOUNTAINS
Elko
Spring Creek
Wells
80
West Wendover
Snow Water Lake
BLACK ROCK DESERT
Quinn River
New Year Lake
Pyramid Lake Indian Reservation
THE LAVA BEDS
Rye Patch Reservoir
Humboldt River
SHOSHONE RANGE
Humboldt-Toiyabe National Forest
Goshute Indian Reservation
South Fork Indian Reservation
Huntington River
93
TRINITY RANGE
Lovelock
278
80
Pyramid Lake
STILLWATER RANGE
Humboldt Salt Marsh
CLAN ALPINE MOUNTAINS
TOIYABE RANGE
Hickison Petroglyph Recreation Area
RUBY MOUNTAINS
Humboldt-Toiyabe National Forest
305
Sparks
Reno
Silver Springs
Fallon
95
Fallon Indian Reservation
Eureka
50
Ely
RUTH COPPER PIT
SNAKE RANGE
Great Basin National Park
Humboldt-Toiyabe National Forest
Carson City
Lake Tahoe
Walker River Indian Reservation
Lahontan Reservoir
MONITOR RANGE
Humboldt-Toiyabe National Forest
Berlin Ichthyosaur State Park
Duckwater Indian Reservation
6
White River
Humboldt-Toiyabe National Forest
Stateline
Topaz Lake
SIERRA NEVADA
Humboldt-Toiyabe National Forest
Walker Lake
Hawthorne
95
376
LUNAR CRATER
93
EXCELSIOR MOUNTAINS
BOUNDARY PEAK
375
Cathedral Gorge State Park
Caliente
Pahranagat National Wildlife Refuge
Tonopah
350
LEVIATHAN CAVE GEOLOGICAL AREA
DELAMAR MOUNTAINS
Meadow Valley Wash
NATIONAL WILDHORSE MANAGEMENT AREA
NEVADA TEST SITE
DESERT NATIONAL WILDLIFE RANGE
SHEEP RANGE
Mesquite
Death Valley National Park
Beatty
Humboldt-Toiyabe National Forest
AMARGOSA DESERT
Mt. Charleston Wilderness Area
Moapa Indian Reservation
Overton
15
Lake Mead National Recreation Area
GYPSUM CAVE
Las Vegas
Lake Mead
Hoover Dam
Pahrump
Henderson
Sandy Valley
95
MOJAVE DESERT
Laughlin
Lake Mohave
Colorado River

miles
0   30

Interstate Highway
U.S. Highway
State Highway
State Capital
City or Town
Wildlife Refuge
Highest Point in the State
Mountains
State Park
National Forest
National Park
Wilderness Area
Indian Reservation
Recreation Area

N E S W

NEVADA
MAP SKILLS

1. What city is nearest Pahranagat National Wildlife Refuge?

2. Which Native American reservation is furthest north?

3. What copper mine is closest to Ely?

4. Which city is on the north end of Lake Mead?

5. Name four cities on the Humboldt River that lie east of Winnemucca.

6. What main highway runs the length of the state north to south, and at one point joins Interstate 80?

7. What desert is northeast of Pyramid Lake?

8. The Shoshone Range is nearest what two highways?

9. Which city is nearer to the state capital, Sparks or Tonopah?

10. Which direction do you have to travel on Highway 50 from Eureka to reach Fallon?

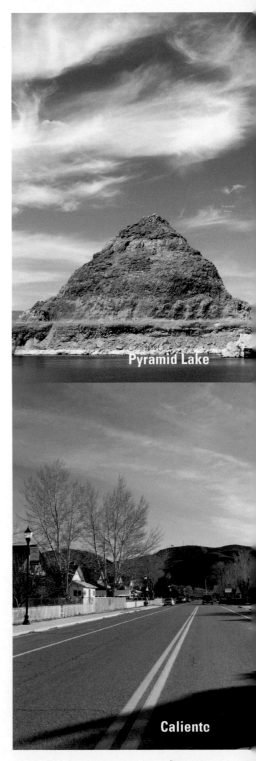

Pyramid Lake

Caliente

10. West
9. Sparks
8. Interstate 80 and Highway 305
7. Black Rock Desert
6. Highway 95
5. Battle Mountain, Elko, Wells, and West Wendover
4. Overton
3. Ruth Copper Pit
2. Fort McDermitt Indian Reservation
1. Caliente

State Flag, Seal, and Song

The Nevada state flag, adopted in 1929 and revised in 1991, has a cobalt-blue background. In the upper left-hand corner sits a five-pointed silver star with the word Nevada in gold below it. Above the star is a gold scroll containing the phrase Battle Born. To the right and left of the star are sprays of sagebrush.

Nevada's state seal, which was officially adopted in 1866, shows the words "The Great Seal of the State of Nevada" in a circle on a cobalt-blue field. Inside the circle is a picture of farm equipment, a mine, and a steam train, with the sun rising above mountains in the background. A scroll beneath the picture bears Nevada's state motto "All for Our Country." Thirty-six stars on the inner circle of the seal represent Nevada as the thirty-sixth state to join the Union.

The Nevada State Song begins with the lyrics "Way out in the land of the setting sun, where the wind blows wild and free, there's a lovely spot that means home to me …"
The state song is titled "Home Means Nevada," with words and music by Bertha Raffetto. Lyrics and origin of the song can be found at: **www.netstate.com/states/symb/song/nv_home_means_nv.htm**

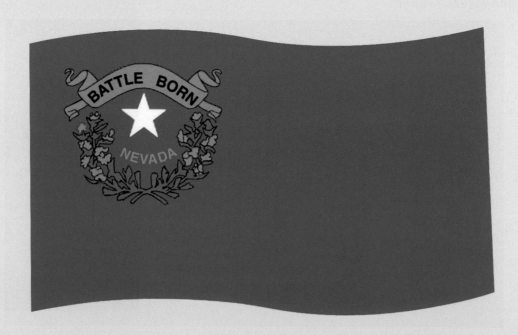

Glossary

conservation   The careful use of natural resources to prevent them from being lost or wasted.

fauna   The animals that are specific to a region, habitat, or geologic period.

flash flood   A flood caused by heavy or excessive rainfall in a short time, usually less than six hours.

flora   The plants that are specific to a region, habitat, or geologic period.

fossil   A preserved remnant of a plant or animal from an older geologic age.

geothermal   Using the natural heat produced inside the Earth; sometimes this comes in the form of very hot water.

granite   A very hard igneous rock that is used as a building stone.

herbivore   An animal that feeds on plants, as opposed to a carnivore, which feeds on animals.

initiative   In government, a procedure where citizens can propose a law and have it put to a vote in an election.

irrigation   A system of pumps, pipes and/or canals that draw fresh water from lakes and rivers and deliver it to crop fields.

munitions   Military weapons, ammunition, and equipment.

paleo   Older or ancient; this term is used especially in describing the geologic past.

referendum   In government, a procedure where citizens can propose to repeal a law and vote to have the repeal approved.

reservation   An area of land in the US that is kept separate as a place for Native Americans to live.

wickiup   A dome-shaped home made of woven grasses, constructed by Native Americans.

More About Nevada

BOOKS

Gabriel, Luke S. *The Hoover Dam*. Mankato, MN: The Child's World, 2015.

Martin, Ted. *Area 51*. Minneapolis, MN: Bellwether Media, 2011.

Sanford, William R. *Kit Carson, Courageous Mountain Man*. New York: Enslow, 2013.

Shull, Jodie A. *Voice of the Paiutes: A Story about Sarah Winnemucca*. Minneapolis, MN: Millbrook Press, 2007.

WEBSITES

Nevada Department of Wildlife

www.ndow.org/Nevada_Wildlife/Animals/

Nevada State Parks

parks.nv.gov

Official Website of the State of Nevada

www.nv.gov

ABOUT THE AUTHORS

Terry Allen Hicks has written books on a wide range of subjects, many of them in the It's My State! series. He lives in Connecticut with his wife and children.

Ellen H. Todras is a freelance writer and editor who lives with her husband in Eugene, Oregon. She loves history, and has written parts of social studies textbooks and other books about the United States.

Ruth Bjorklund lives on an island near Seattle, Washington, and enjoys exploring the western United States. She has contributed to many titles in the It's My State! series.

Index

Page numbers in **boldface** are illustrations. Entries in **boldface** are glossary terms.

Index